Colorado

Luther Library
Midland University
Fremont, NE 68025

Wildflowers

A beginner's
field guide to
the state's most
common flowers

D1501752

Interpreting the Great Outdoors

Text by Charlotte Foltz Jones, Illustrations by DD Dowden

FALCON

582.13
V 712c

For Mildred Foltz,
who first showed me the flowers

Interpreting the Great Outdoors

Nature's wonders, such as the wildflowers, are certainly remarkable, but unfortunately many people—especially young people—know little about them. That's one reason Falcon Press has launched this series of books called Interpreting the Great Outdoors.

Other books in the series include *The Tree Giants: The Story of the Redwoods, the World's Largest Trees; The Fire Mountains: The Story of the Cascade Volcanoes; Montana Wildlife; Where Dinosaurs Still Rule; California Wildflowers; Arizona Wildflowers; Oregon Wildflowers; Minnesota Wildflowers; Montana Wildflowers; North Carolina Wildflowers;* and *Texas Wildflowers.*

To get extra copies of this book or others in the series, please visit your local bookstore, or write to Falcon Press, P.O. Box 1718, Helena, MT 59624. Or call toll-free 1-800-582-2665. Falcon Press publishes and distributes a wide variety of books and calendars, so be sure to ask for our free catalog.

Copyright © 1994
by Falcon Press Publishing Co., Inc.,
Billings and Helena, Montana.

All rights reserved, including the right to reproduce any part of this book in any form, with the exception of brief quotations included in a review, without the written permission of the publisher.

The author would like to thank Miriam Denham, Ph.D., who served as botanical consultant; Denver Botanical Gardens; Libbie Landreth, Great Sand Dunes National Monument; James A. Mack, Rocky Mountain National Park; Linda Martin, Mesa Verde National Park; and David Whitman, Dinosaur National Monument.

Design, editing, typesetting, and other prepress work by Falcon Press, Helena, Montana. Printed in Hong Kong.

Library of Congress Cataloging-in-Publication Data

Jones, Charlotte.
    Colorado wildflowers : a beginner's field guide to the state's
most common flowers / text by Charlotte Jones : illustrations by DD
Dowden.
            p.   cm. – (Interpreting the great outdoors)
    Includes index.
    ISBN 1-56044-266-2
    1. Wild flowers–Colorado–Identification.   2. Wild flowers-
-Colorado–Pictorial works.   I. Title.   II. Title : Colorado wild
flowers.   III. Series.
QK150.J65   1994   **28990**   94-6075
582.13'09788–dc20   CIP

Contents

Introduction

Coyotes run. Birds fly. Fish swim.

Plants, however, can't move from place to place. And they can't call out for pizza. Fortunately, they *can* collect everything they need to survive—sunlight, water, air, and nutrients from the soil—without ever budging an inch. They absorb all these things through their leaves and roots. No *animal* can make such a claim!

Plants are fascinating life forms. The scientists who study them are called botanists, but you don't have to be a botanist to enjoy and learn more about plants and flowers. This book will give you a glimpse of what an interesting and pleasurable hobby the study of wildflowers can be.

Before you rush out to gather wildflowers, remember that picking them is illegal in many areas of Colorado! You're likely to see signs to this effect at park entrances or trailheads on public land. If you pick wildflowers on private land, be certain you have permission from the landowner.

One good reason *not* to pick wildflowers is that the plants that inhabit an area determine what kinds of wildlife live there. The number of plants determines how many of those animals will survive. When people change the plant life in an area, they also change the animal life—whether they mean to or not.

Another reason not to pick wildflowers is so that more people can have the chance to enjoy them. Imagine hiking along a trail behind someone who's already picked every flower in sight!

The fact is, you don't need to pick flowers to study them. Instead, keep a flower notebook. Draw the blossoms you find. When you go for a walk or a hike, take along a box of colored pencils. A magnifying glass and a pair of tweezers will help you examine a plant more closely. When you draw a flower, you become aware of all its intricate parts.

In the following pages, you'll see that each wildflower has one or more common names—Colorado blue columbine, for example. Each also has a scientific name, usually in Latin—in this case *Aquilegia caerulea.* The first part of the scientific name tells you what genus the plant belongs to. The second part gets more specific. It tells you the plant's species.

Some of the flowers in this book are what people often call "weeds." They grow in vacant lots, beside fences, or along roadsides. They're unplanned and unwanted—just like a bean plant in a row of lettuce or a poppy in a rose garden.

The dictionary says a weed is "a plant of no value." But almost every plant serves some purpose. Its roots might help hold the soil in place and keep it from eroding, or break up hard-packed soil so that other plants can thrive. It might provide protection or food for some kinds of wildlife. Or it might simply provide a spot of beauty in an otherwise drab landscape. Weeds, you might say, are in the eye of the beholder!

Some of the plants in this book have been used as food—by animals or by people, especially Native Americans. But do *not* taste or eat these plants! There are several reasons:

   * Some poisonous plants look much like non-poisonous ones. Often, only experts can tell the difference.

   * You would have to pick a wildflower to eat it, and this isn't a good idea for the reasons given above.

   * Some non-poisonous plants may become poisonous if they grow in soil that has been contaminated.

   * Some plants edible by animals are poisonous to humans.

Certainly you don't need to taste a wildflower to appreciate it. Instead, sniff its fragrance. Open your eyes to its beauty. Reach out and touch it gently.

There are more than five thousand species of wildflowers in Colorado. Just think of the pleasure that awaits you!

Multiple Life Zones

Do you know why Denver is called the Mile-High City? It's because Denver is 5,280 feet—one mile—above sea level. That's its altitude.

Colorado's climate is determined by altitude. For instance, on the Fourth of July it might be ninety degrees Fahrenheit in Denver but thirty degrees on top of Trail Ridge Road in Rocky Mountain National Park. The altitude there is 12,183 feet above sea level.

Plant life grows in layers of altitude that scientists call "life zones." These layers don't have sharp boundaries but tend to overlap each other. There are five such zones in Colorado: the plains, foothills, montane, subalpine, and alpine. Many plants grow in more than one of them.

Here are some of the wildflowers that grow in at least four of Colorado's five life zones. Remember that the plant's size, blooming season, and even color can be affected by different elevations, climates, amounts of rainfall, soil conditions, and especially whether the growing location (called the "exposure") faces north or south.

Yellow Stonecrop

other names: Orpine, Lance-Leaved Stonecrop
height: 2-5 inches
season: June-August

Don't expect this flower to stand tall and wave at you! Look close to the ground to find the yellow stonecrop. Its name seems appropriate since you'll see it in dry, rocky ground from the plains up to the alpine zone. Notice its leaves. The waxy coating helps prevent water loss. The plant can survive dry periods by lying dormant, then growing again when water is plentiful.

Sedum lanceolatum

Mountain Candytuft

other names: Mountain Pennycress, Wild Candytuft
height: 1-5 inches
season: throughout the summer

"Candytuft" sounds like a delicious sweet that's hard to chew. Unfortunately for candy lovers, this plant got its name simply because it resembles the candytuft people grow in gardens—not because it tastes good. These small plants grow from foothills to mountaintops. Look for them in thin soil on or around rocks, often near clusters of spruce trees. This is an early spring flower in the foothills. Sometimes it blooms near snowbanks at higher elevations.

Thlaspi montanum

Harebell

other names: Mountain Bellflower, Bluebell
height: 4-12 inches, 2-3 inches at timberline
season: June-September, depending on location and elevation

The genus name, *Campanula*, is from the Latin for "little bell," and this flower truly looks like it has little bells hanging downward to protect its pollen from the rain. *Rotundifolia* means "round leaves," but you'll find these only at the base of the stem. The stem leaves are long and narrow. This flower is considered a symbol of constancy and kindness.

Campanula rotundifolia

Yarrow

other names: Milfoil, Tansy
height: 6-10 inches
season: June-August

The mythological Greek hero Achilles used yarrow leaves to treat his soldiers' wounds—hence the genus name, *Achillea*. At one time yarrow was thought to be a witch's herb! Native Americans and early western settlers used it as a cure for fevers. They also boiled the fernlike leaves to make tea. If a cow grazes on yarrow (which it would rather not), its milk will taste terrible! The plant has an interesting odor, too. Look for yarrow in all the zones from the plains to the alpine peaks.

Tansy Aster

other names: none
height: 1-3 feet
season: August-September

Asters look a lot like daisies. But the aster's ray flowers (what a lot of people call "petals") are wider, and there are fewer of them. Daisies bloom earlier in the summer, while asters bloom closer to fall. Look for the tansy aster along roadsides or on disturbed ground from the plains up to the subalpine zone. Notice how the leaflike bracts beneath the flower head are sticky and curl downward.

Machaeranthera bigelovii

other names: Paintbrush
height: 12-36 inches
season: May-September

Usually small, modified leaves called "bracts" circle the base of a flower, and its petals are large and colorful. But not in the Indian paintbrush! It has many colorful bracts at the tip of the "flower." The real petals (joined together to form a tube) are green and hidden so that you can hardly see them. Look for various species of different colors: red, orange, rosy pink, maroon, crimson, and yellow. Paintbrushes are semi-parasitic. This means that their roots steal food from the roots of other plants. One type of paintbrush is Wyoming's state flower.

Achillea lanulosa

Castilleja sp.

Plains

Hot summers. Cold winters. Lots of sunshine. Long periods of drought. Those are the conditions that plants must cope with on the Colorado plains. This land, generally flat with an elevation below 5,500 feet, can be found east of the Rocky Mountains and in several large pockets in the western part of the state.

It's amazing how many flowering plants can grow under these extreme conditions. In general, they do so by using one or more of the following survival techniques:

* They have a short life cycle from seed to seed.
* They conserve root moisture by having few leaves.
* They have thorny or tough leaves that animals won't eat.
* They spend the dry, hot months as a dormant bulb or buried root.

Prickly Pear

other names: none
height: up to 15 inches
season: May-June

Mickey Mouse ears! That's what more than one person has called the jointed stems and round, spiny pads of the prickly pear cactus. Cacti can withstand long periods without water. Their tissue absorbs water when it's plentiful, and a thick layer of wax prevents it from evaporating. The prickly pear's fruit is delicious when cooked, in jelly, or as a candy. But first the spines must be removed by peeling away the outer rind. Prickly pear flowers can be yellow, orange, rust, red, or purple. Look quickly! Most cactus blossoms only last for a day or two.

Easter Daisy

other names: none
height: 3 inches
season: April-June

We know spring has arrived when the Easter daisies bloom! This is one of the earliest flowers to blossom on the plains—often during the Easter season. That's how it got its common name. You might also find this daisy in the foothills. But look closely! It grows very close to the ground.

Rabbit Brush

other names: False Goldenrod, Goldenbush
height: 1-4 feet
season: July-September

This shrub thrives on land where other plants can't live. Look for it on roadsides, dry slopes, and waste areas of the dry plains and up into the foothills. The plant contains rubber, but not enough for companies to make money processing it. The flowers can be used to make a yellow dye for cloth. Rabbit brush provides shelter for animals. There might be a rabbit watching you from inside the shrubbery!

Chrysothamnus nauseosus

Opuntia macrorhiza

Townsendia hookeri var. exscapa

Prickly Poppy

other names: none
height: 15 inches to 5 feet
season: May-September

"Prickly" is certainly the right word to describe this plant! It has spiny leaves on the stem. The flower's six petals look as though they might be made of delicate white paper. The leaves and seeds of the prickly poppy are extremely poisonous. Animals won't eat any part of the plant. In a few rare cases, the seeds from the prickly poppy have mixed with wheat and corn during harvesting. When humans ate the grains, they became very ill. Doves, however, can eat the prickly poppy seeds with no ill effects. Many people say that when the prickly poppy starts blooming, you know summer has arrived. Look for the prickly poppy along roadsides and on dry slopes.

Salsify

other names: Goat Dandelion, Goatsbeard
height: 12-18 inches
season: June-July

Here's a flower that's more noticeable after it goes to seed, when it looks like a tall, very large dandelion. The plant has a leafy stem, and the leaves are narrow and linear. Native Americans used the plant's milky juice to treat indigestion. Salsify grows in waste places and along roadsides. Its yellow flowers bloom in the morning and close by noon. A close relative is the oyster plant, which has a large taproot, but it has purple flowers instead of yellow.

Showy Milkweed

other names: Pink Milkweed, Silkweed
height: 18 inches to 6 feet
season: June-July

Look for showy milkweed in clumps beside streams or ditches and near roadsides. Most species of milkweed are poisonous, but Native Americans cooked the shoots, leaves, buds, flowers, and seed pods of this non-poisonous species. The young shoots taste like asparagus. This plant has been used in medicine for centuries. The name milkweed refers to the milky juice called latex that oozes from the plant's cut stem.

Argemone polyanthemos

Tragopogon dubius

Asclepias speciosa

9

Foothills

You'll find more wildflowers in the foothills than in any other life zone. The region is hospitable because it gets more rain than the plains. The hills and valleys offer protection from storms. And the soil washed down from higher land or left by ancient glaciers is more favorable for growing.

The foothills generally are defined as land between 5,500 and 8,000 feet in elevation. Many of the wildflowers found on the plains also grow higher into these hills, and other species found in the higher mountains reach downward, especially along stream banks.

Rocky Mountain Phlox

other names: Rockhill Phlox,
    Spreading Phlox
height: 8-12 inches
season: May-July

Multiflora means "many flowers," which describes this phlox well. Sniff its sweet smell! Phlox has become a very popular plant for people to grow in gardens. In the Colorado foothills, Rocky Mountain phlox grows on shrubby slopes and can be white to light blue or light pink to lavender.

Pasque Flower

other names: Prairie Smoke, Wild
    Crocus, many more
height: 2-16 inches
season: March-June

The pasque flower is named for *Paques*, the French word for "Easter," because that's when it usually appears. Sometimes the plant will poke through the snow to bloom. The pasque flower is the state flower of South Dakota. It contains an oil used to make some medicines. It doesn't make a good forage plant for animals, and sheep have died from overfeeding on it.

Oregon Grape

other names: Creeping Barberry,
    Mountain Holly
height: up to 15 inches
season: April-June

This plant isn't holly, and it isn't a grape. It creeps along the ground on dry, open hillsides and rocky slopes. It spreads because of underground stems, and its name, *repens*, means "creeping." Its spiny, hollylike leaves turn red, purple, or yellow in the fall. Deer and elk seldom eat this plant, but black bears eat the blue berries. Native Americans also ate the berries and made a yellow clothing dye from the dried stems and roots. Oregon chose another species of this plant (*Mahonia aquifolium*) as its state flower.

Pulsatilla patens

Mahonia repens

Phlox multiflora

Pussytoes

other names: Cat's Paws, Everlasting
height: 2-8 inches
season: June-August

Anyone who likes cats will understand how this plant got its name. Each flower head is very small, and it looks and feels like the toes of a kitten. Native Americans chewed a gum made from the stalks of some species of this plant. Look for pussytoes in moist meadows and valleys and on mountainsides. The plants grow in a mat and might cover a patch several feet wide. Unlike most cats, pussytoes like to put their feet in water!

Antennaria
rosea

False Solomon's Seal

other names: Wild Lily of the
    Valley, Wild Spikenard
height: 12-24 inches
season: May-July

Why "false?" Because the "true" Solomon's seal (*Polygonatum* spp.) has similar growing habits and a similar leaf shape, but its flowers hang from the underside of the stem like clothes from a clothesline. The flowers of the false Solomon's seal form a cone-shaped spray at the end of the stem. The plant grows best in moist woods and meadows, as well as along valley streams. Its roots grow horizontally, allowing the plant to grow in groups. When the plant is young, the leaves and shoots can be eaten as a green vegetable. Elk also enjoy the leaves and stems.

Blanket Flower

other names: Gaillardia, Brown-Eyed
    Susan
height: 10-30 inches
season: June-August

This is an easy flower to identify because of its reddish-brown or maroon center. The Latin name *aristata* means "bearded" and refers to the hairy receptacle of the flowering head. The common name blanket flower was given because the plant inspired Native American women to weave its design into their blankets and because the plants spread out and interweave until they look like a colorful blanket. The common name brown-eyed Susan (or black-eyed Susan) has been loosely attached to many other wildflowers.

Smilacina stellata

Gaillardia
aristata

11

Foothills continued

Beebalm

other names: Horsemint, Wild
Bergamot
height: 1-2 feet
season: June-August

Look for this plant along damp roadsides and in moist, open meadows. It usually grows in clumps. As the name suggests, it's a popular flower with bees. *Menthifolia* means "mint-leaved." The leaves of this plant can be used to make tea or as a seasoning in cooking. The oil of the plant contains a small amount of antiseptic. Cattle and wild game eat beebalm, but horses don't care for it.

Monarda fistulosa
var. *menthifolia*

Goldenrod

other names: Yellowweed
height: 1-6 feet
season: July-September

Many people associate the goldenrod with going back-to-school. When the plant begins to bloom, it's a signal that summer is ending. Goldenrod likes to grow in moist soil along fences and highways and in open woods or waste areas. Animals seldom eat the plant, which contains a small amount of rubber. Kentucky and Nebraska selected species of the goldenrod as their state flowers.

Solidago sp.

Spring Beauty

other names: Groundnut,
Lanceleaf Spring Beauty
height: 2-6 inches
season: April-June

The spring beauty is one of the earliest plants to bloom each year. A few people have reported seeing blossoms in January! Look for the spring beauty on mesas, along the edges of woods, and below snowbanks. While this species is more common on the western slope, a similar species, *Claytonia rosea*, is common along the front range. Native Americans ate the spring beauty's corm, a thick, underground stem similar to a tuber. It tastes a little like a radish when raw and like potato when boiled.

Grizzly bears and rodents love the corm. Deer, elk, and sheep graze on the upper part of the plant. *Lanceolata* means that the leaves are lance-shaped— long, narrow, and widest at the base.

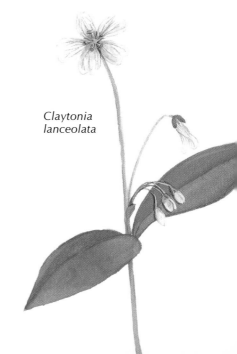

*Claytonia
lanceolata*

Sulphur Flower

other names: Umbrella Plant
height: 4-15 inches
season: June-August

You might need a magnifying glass to examine the sulphur flower. Why the common name "umbrella?" Look at the way the flower stalks (peduncles) grow from a common point—sort of like umbrella ribs. The clusters of tiny flowers are also on short umbrella-like stalks. If you have permission to pick sulphur flowers, they can be dried and used as a winter bouquet. The plant makes an excellent honey, and sheep prefer it to other forage. Native Americans used the sulphur flower to treat many ailments.

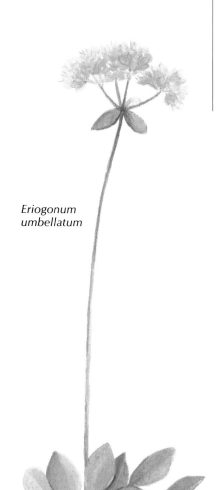

Eriogonum umbellatum

Western Wallflower

other names: Blister Cress
height: 8-24 inches
season: July-August

The mustard you spread on a sandwich is made from a member of this flower's family. Native Americans used the seeds of this plant as flavoring for food. Look for the western wallflower in open pine forests and open meadows, along streams, near spruce trees, and along roadsides. Also look near rocks or stone walls. That's how this plant got the common name "wallflower."

Erysimum asperum

Shooting Star

other names: Birdbill
height: 6-16 inches
season: June-July

Imagine a flower shooting through space! With its rose-colored, backward-curved petals and its black nose pointing skyward, this blossom almost seems to have sparks trailing behind it! The genus name *Dodecatheon* comes from two Greek words meaning "twelve" and "gods." A Greek legend claims that this flower was so beautiful it needed twelve gods to protect it. Elk, deer, and cattle graze on the tender shoots of the young plant, which can be found in wet meadows and by stream banks.

Dodecatheon pulchellum

Montane Zone

Here, where the altitude is between eight thousand and ten thousand feet, about twice as much rain falls as on the plains. But flowers that grow in this mountainous region do have to overcome a few disadvantages: a fairly short growing season; less sunshine because of tree shade; competition with tree and shrub roots for nutrients in the soil; and steep, rocky hillsides.

Columbine

other names: Colorado Blue
   Columbine
height: 8-24 inches
season: July-August

The columbine has been Colorado's state flower since 1899. The blue color in the blossom is a symbol for Colorado's blue skies, the white is for the snow, and the gold is for the rich metal that started the 1859 gold rush to the area. The genus name *Aquilegia* is from a Latin word that means "eagle," and the spurs on the flowers do look a little like an eagle's talons. The common name columbine is from the Latin word for "dove." Do you think the blossom looks a bit like the heads of several doves? Red and yellow species of columbine also grow in Colorado.

Yellow Monkeyflower

other names: Wild Lettuce
height: 4-18 inches
season: May-August

Its unusual, somewhat monkeylike shape earned this flower its name. The genus name *Mimulus* means "mask." Some say the monkeyflower's face looks a little like the tragedy/comedy masks of the ancient Greek theater. Others claim the dots of color on the lobes of some of the species look like a face. Native Americans and early western settlers ate the bitter leaves of this plant much as we eat lettuce.

Shrubby Cinquefoil

other names: Yellow Rose,
   Fivefingers
height: 1-3 feet
season: June-August

Domestic and wild animals will eat this shrub, although they don't prefer it. Since it keeps its leaves during the winter, it provides nourishment for big game animals when food is scarce. The cinquefoil is a useful "indicator plant." When it's over-browsed, a rancher knows he has too much livestock on the range. Over-browsing on a game range warns a wildlife biologist that herds are too big and hunting should be increased. *Cinque* is French for "five." Many cinquefoils have five leaflets. This plant is often used to landscape yards.

Mimulus guttatus

Aquilegia caerulea

Potentilla fruticosa

Fireweed

other names: Blooming Sally,
  Willowherb
height: 1-5 feet
season: July-September

After a forest fire, the fireweed is a welcome sight. It's one of the first plants to grow and cover the scarred land. Fireweed helps hold the soil in place and provides food for wildlife. It also grows well in disturbed ground along roadsides. Native Americans used the leaves to make tea, and in the spring they boiled and ate the new shoots. Elk, deer, and domestic livestock also like to eat the plant. It's a favorite of grizzly bears.

Epilobium angustifolium

Death Camas

other names: Wand Lily, Poison
  Sego
height: 8-18 inches
season: June-August

If death camas sounds like a scary name, it should! This plant is very poisonous to humans and livestock. Hogs, however, seem to be immune to the poison. *Zigadenus* is Greek for "yoked gland," referring to the two glands near the base of each of the six tepals. *Elegans* means "fine" or "elegant." That's certainly a fitting description of this elegant—though deadly—member of the lily family.

Mountain Gentian

other names: Parry Gentian, Blue
  Gentian
height: 6-15 inches
season: August-September

Look for the mountain gentian in moist meadows, along stream banks, and in bogs. Ancient Greeks and Romans, as well as many other cultures throughout history, used gentian as a medicine. In Colorado, early settlers used the clear, bitter fluid of the mountain gentian as a tonic. This flower is also called Parry gentian in honor of Charles C. Parry, an English doctor who first visited Colorado in 1861. Many wildflowers carry his name.

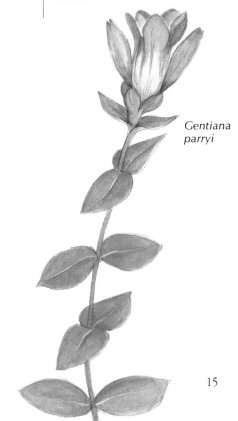

Gentiana parryi

Zigadenus elegans

15

Subalpine Zone

High in the mountains, above ten thousand feet, winter snows tend to linger—especially on slopes facing north where there's little sun. Here in the subalpine zone, which extends up to 11,500 feet, it's common to have frost in the middle of the summer. Since the growing season is so short, the time between the blooming of a plant and the ripening of its seeds must be short, too. So you'll have to move quickly to see wildflowers blossoming here.

You might find some alpine plants growing in the meadows of the subalpine zone.

Red Anemone

other names: Windflower
height: 10-12 inches
season: June-July

Multifida means "many cleft" and refers to the shape of the leaves. The seeds develop in a hairy cluster. Most species of this genus are believed to contain a poison that affects the nervous system. Native Americans thought the anemone had strong healing powers and used the roots to treat wounds. Deer and elk occasionally eat this plant. It's fairly common, but it grows in partial shade and, because it's small, is not as showy as some other flowers. You may have to look closely to find it.

Anemone multifida var. *globosa*

Dogtooth Violet

other names: Avalanche Lily, Snow Lily
height: 6-18 inches
season: July-August

This plant is *not* a violet—it's a lily. Native Americans boiled and ate the bulb of this plant. Grizzly and black bears and small rodents also eat the bulbs. The green seed pods are eaten by deer, elk, and bighorn sheep. The dogtooth violet can be found in moist meadows, growing in large patches near melting snowdrifts —often under aspen trees.

Erythronium grandiflorum

Twinflower

other names: none
height: 2-4 inches
season: June-August

In 1737, a Swedish man named Carolus Linnaeus developed a way to classify all plants and animals by giving them each a two-part scientific name: first, a generic name (genus), and second, a specific name (species). We still use his system today. This particular flower was named *Linnaea* in his honor because it was his favorite. Its common name, twinflower, comes from the two bell-shaped flowers on each stem. This plant grows in moist, shaded areas, usually under trees. It's not an easy plant to find.

Linnaea borealis

Monkshood

other names: Aconite
height: 2-5 feet
season: June-August

This is an unusual flower with an unusual name. Its two tiny petals are hidden under a hood formed by the blue or violet sepals. Apparently some people thought the flower resembled the hood worn by religious monks. A European species of this plant called wolfbane has been used to ward off werewolves! All parts of this plant are poisonous. One of the poisons in the plant— aconite—was once used to make a medicine to lower fevers.

*Aconitum
columbianum*

Globeflower

other names: none
height: 10-18 inches
season: May-August

Look for the globeflower in marshy areas and wet meadows, near melting snowbanks, and along stream banks. It often grows near marsh marigolds, and the two plants look much alike. The most obvious difference is in the leaves. Those of the marsh marigold are dark, waxy green, and their base is heart-shaped. The globeflower's leaves are smaller and have toothed edges and five lobes. The genus name, *Trollius*, is from the German word *trollblume*, which means "globelike flower."

Parry Lousewort

other names: none
height: 4-12 inches
season: July-August

Does lousewort sound like a strange name for a flower? People once believed that livestock that ate this plant would get lice. Later, people used the seeds of the lousewort to try to rid themselves of head lice. *Parryi* indicates that this flower is named for Charles Parry, a nineteenth-century botanist. Look for Parry lousewort on open slopes and in meadows. Notice that the flowers seem to have two lips. The upper lip forms a curved beak.

*Pedicularis
parryi*

*Trollius laxus
var. albiflorus*

17

Subalpine continued

King's Crown

other names: Roseroot
height: 4-12 inches
season: June-August

The genus name *Sedum* comes from the Latin word *sedo* or *sedeo*, which means "to sit." This refers to the way some members of this genus attach themselves to rocks and walls. The dark red flower of the king's crown makes it easy to differentiate from a similar plant, the rose crown (sometimes called queen's crown). The rose crown's flowers are a delicate pink, and the plant often grows beside a lake or other water. King's crown likes drier ground and might be found near cliffs or on ridges. Its common name, roseroot, comes from its roselike fragrance. Its young leaves and stems can be eaten raw or cooked.

Snowball Saxifrage

other names: Diamond Leaf
   Saxifrage
height: 2-12 inches
season: May-July

Saxifrage means "rock breaker" and refers to the fact that this plant grows in cracks in rocks and can actually force a rock apart. People used to believe it could also break up kidney stones. The snowball saxifrage can often be found in early spring at lower elevations, but it blooms in midsummer in the subalpine zone. Look in moist places for this interesting plant with the flat rosette of leaves at its base and the tall, leafless stem topped by a cluster or ball of white flowers.

Triangle-Leaved Ragwort

other names: Arrowleaf Groundsel
height: 1-5 feet
season: July-August

This tall plant grows along stream banks, often in such large numbers that it camouflages the stream. Look for the triangular, or arrow-shaped, leaves. The Latin word *senecio* means "old man," and refers to the white hairs common to some species in this genus.

Senecio triangularis

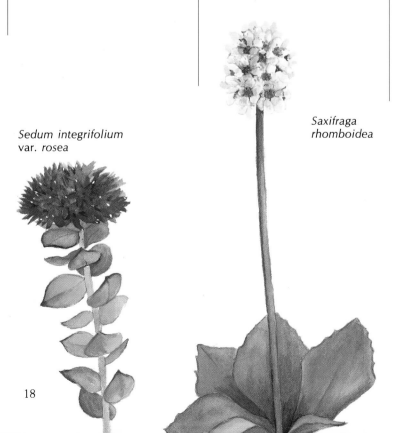

Sedum integrifolium
var. *rosea*

Saxifraga
rhomboidea

Parry Primrose

other names: Alpine Primrose
height: 10 inches to 2 feet
season: July-August

Growing in rock crevices, meadows, and bogs, along stream banks, and in other wet areas, Parry primrose owes its intense magenta color to a chemical in the plant called anthocyanin. Many plants at higher elevations have more intense color because the thin air there allows more sunlight to penetrate. Parry primrose has a very unpleasant odor, but that and its bright color are what attract the insects needed to pollinate the plant.

Pearly Everlasting

other names: Life-Everlasting, Indian Tobacco
height: 12-18 inches
season: July-August

If you have permission to pick this wildflower, you can dry it and use it in long-lasting floral arrangements. It won't lose its color or form. The pearly everlasting is common along roadsides and trails, as well as on land that has recently been burned. Be sure to notice the leaves of this plant. They're green on top but white with soft, woolly hairs underneath.

Purple Fringe

other names: Purple Pincushion, Scorpionweed
height: 4-12 inches
season: July-August

Purple fringe is common along roadsides and in rocky or disturbed soils. From a bit of a distance, its dark purple stalk looks fringed. Up close, you'll notice that each "fringe" is actually a stamen tipped with orange-yellow pollen sacs. The purple fringe has an unpleasant odor. Elk and other big game don't seem to notice and enjoy grazing on it.

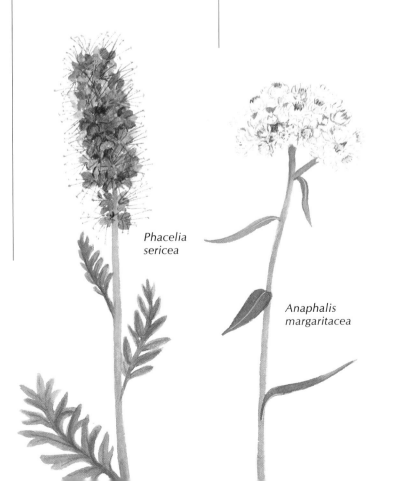

Phacelia sericea

Anaphalis margaritacea

Primula parryi

Alpine Zone

The alpine zone begins where the trees end—at timberline. The climate here is severe, with cold temperatures, strong winds, and frost or even snow during the summer. Trees can't withstand such a harsh climate. Yet, the alpine slopes are a "garden" of wildflowers.

Why? Strange as it may seem, there are some advantages to growing at this high altitude: rich soil, adequate precipitation, and no trees to block the sunlight. Alpine plants have adapted to the difficult conditions in several ways. They have no stems or short stems, so they hug the ground; smaller leaves that offer less resistance to the wind; long roots to keep them from being ripped away by the wind; and fine hairs or waxy leaves to conserve moisture. Many alpine plants are perennials, which means they last from year to year instead of going to seed and dying each year as annuals do.

Moss Campion

other names: Cushion Pink
height: only 0.5-1 inch, but often a
    foot or more across
season: June-August

This isn't a true moss, but it looks something like one with its narrow, needlelike leaves. The moss campion doesn't bloom until it's ten years old. It might reach a foot in diameter by the age of twenty-five. Maybe this is what's meant by a "late-bloomer!" This plant has no stem, but it has a sturdy taproot to help hold it in place at the summit of a windy, treeless peak.

Marsh Marigold

other names: Elk's Lip,
    Meadowbright
height: 3-10 inches
season: June-August

Not surprisingly, you should look in marshy areas for the marsh marigold. Sometimes it's so anxious to bloom that it pushes its way up through the snow. The white parts of this flower look like petals, but they're actually sepals. Notice the dark, shiny, heart-shaped leaves. Although this plant is believed to be poisonous to cattle, elk feast on it.

Alpine Spring Beauty

other names: Big-Rooted Spring
    Beauty
height: 3-5 inches
season: July-August

This flower might be tiny, but it's tough. It grows in gravelly soil, among rocks, and in rocky crevices. The plant has an amazing root system. The carrot-shaped taproot is one to three inches in diameter and as much as six feet long! At this high altitude, animals and insects are less of a threat than cold, wind, and lack of moisture.

*Caltha
leptosepala*

Silene acaulis

*Claytonia
megarhiza*

Bistort

other names: Snakeweed, Knotweed
height: up to 12 inches
season: July-August

Bistort grows along stream banks and in wet meadows. It has no petals, but its five sepals are petal-like. While each individual flower is tiny, the clusters can be showy. The common name snakeweed comes from the plant's long, twisted root. Knotweed refers to the knobs on the red stem, which make it resemble a fishing pole. The Cheyenne and Blackfeet used bistort in soups. Black bears, grizzly bears, and rodents eat the roots, and deer and elk eat the leaves.

Sky Pilot

other names: Skunkweed
height: 4-12 inches
season: June-August

You'll know why this plant earned the common name skunkweed if you step on one while hiking. The skunklike odor from the crushed leaves will still be on your shoes when you get home in the evening. Sticky hairs that cover the leaves and stem are the source of this memorable aroma. The flowers themselves have a sweet, pleasant smell. Look for sky pilots among rocks.

Snow Buttercup

other names: Alpine Buttercup
height: 4-12 inches
season: June-July

Here's the first flower to bloom in the alpine zone each spring! Usually found at the edge of snowbanks, the snow buttercup will sometimes shoot right up through the snow. Partly opened blooms have even been discovered under twelve feet of snow! Deer, elk, and pikas eat the leaves of the plant. Mice and chipmunks eat the seeds. Most buttercups are poisonous, so don't *you* try to eat them. The species name, *adoneus*, is Greek for "beautiful" or "handsome." That certainly describes the snow buttercup!

Polemonium viscosum

Polygonum bistortoides

Ranunculus adoneus

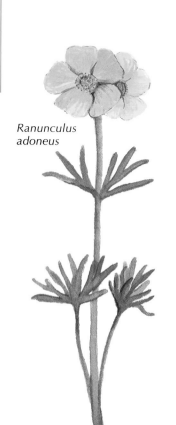

21

Dinosaur National Monument

Extreme. That one word describes the climate in this semidesert country on the Utah-Colorado border. In the winter, the temperature may drop to thirty degrees below zero. In the summer, it may climb to more than one hundred degrees. Only about ten inches of rain fall each year.

Although the Dinosaur Quarry Center in Utah is the monument's biggest draw, there is more to see. The monument covers 326 square miles. Birds are plentiful here, but most avoid the heat of the day and appear at sunset. Animals are difficult to see since most are small, shy, and nocturnal.

Plants must adapt to the harsh conditions. In addition to the following wildflowers, look for greasewood, pinyon, juniper, and sagebrush on the high plateaus above the canyons. On the higher mountainsides, you'll find aspen, Douglas-fir, ponderosa pine, and mountain-mahogany.

Scarlet Gilia

other names: Skyrocket Gilia, Fairy Trumpet
height: 12-36 inches
season: July-August

The scarlet gilia has been called the most unique wildflower in Colorado because of its beauty and bright scarlet color and because so many plants might cover one area. The flowers are trumpet-shaped, flaring at the mouth into five narrow lobes. This plant lives only two years. In the first, there's only a cluster, or rosette, of leaves on the ground. The stem and flowers shoot up in the second year. Another common name, skunk flower, refers to a sticky substance on the stems and leaves that give the plant a skunklike smell.

Sego Lily

other names: Mariposa Lily
height: 8-18 inches
season: June-July

When the Mormons arrived in Utah in 1847, the Utes showed them how to eat the bulb of the sego lily. It tastes a little like potato. Since the plant helped save the Mormons from hunger, it was named Utah's state flower. Another name for this flower, *mariposa*, means "butterfly" in Spanish. When early Spanish explorers saw the breeze blowing across the plains, they thought the flowers looked like fluttering butterflies. Look for the sego lily on dry slopes and open plains.

Locoweed

other names: Milkvetch, Poison Vetch
height: 10-24 inches
season: May-July

Several plants share the name locoweed. Some are members of the genus *Astragalus*. Others belong to the genus *Oxytropis*. Many are poisonous. The name locoweed comes from the Spanish word *loco*, which means "crazy." When animals (especially horses) eat it, they become addicted to it, "go crazy," and eventually die.

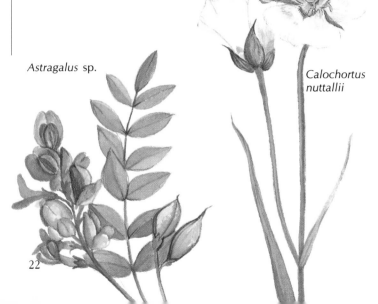

Astragalus sp.

Calochortus nuttallii

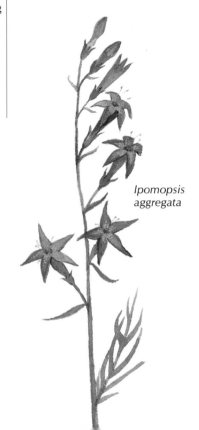

Ipomopsis aggregata

22

Rocky Mountain Bee Plant

other names: Stinkweed, Spider Flower
height: 1-4 feet
season: July-August

The name stinkweed gives you a hint about this flower's aroma! You'll find the plant in sandy areas, along roads, or on overgrazed or waste land. Native Americans boiled and ate the leaves and flowers, which taste a little like mustard. Early Pueblo Indians used nectar from the plant to make black designs on pottery. Bees also find the nectar attractive.

Cleome serrulata

Cowboy's Delight

other names: Scarlet Falsemallow, Copper Mallow
height: 8-12 inches
season: June-August

Look for clusters of this flower along roadsides, in disturbed areas, and on dry plains and mesas. It looks something like a hollyhock. The flowers are usually tomato-red but can also be salmon- or tangerine-colored. The Latin species name, *coccinea*, means "scarlet." The leaves of the cowboy's delight are covered with small, forked hairs, which make them appear a light gray. The plants are a great snack for mule deer and bighorn sheep.

Sphaeralcea coccinea

Lupine

other names: Bluebonnet, Wolfbean
height: 12-30 inches
season: June-August

The name lupine comes from the Latin word for wolf—*lupus*. People once believed that lupines stole nutrients from the soil, just as wolves stole food. We now know the plant actually enriches the soil with nitrogen. (The wolf, too, has a better reputation today.) Through the years, the lupine has been used as a digestive aid, a facial skin cleanser, and a dye for cloth. The Texas bluebonnet, a member of this genus, is the state flower of Texas.

Lupinus sp.

Mesa Verde National Park

The Anasazi left this region seven hundred years ago, leaving behind the spectacular cliff dwellings that are the highlight of the park. Some believe lack of rainfall was one of the reasons the place was abandoned. This area is considered semi-arid. It gets only eighteen inches of precipitation a year. The plants that live here have adapted to this shortage of moisture.

In addition to the wildflowers described here, be sure to look for the Indian paintbrush and lupine, which are also plentiful in the park. They're described elsewhere in this book.

Eaton's Penstemon

other names: Firecracker Penstemon,
  Scarlet Bugler
height: 15-24 inches
season: May-June

"Firecracker" is a good description of this showy flower, since it looks a little like something you'd see on the Fourth of July. Usually found in dry, rocky areas hemmed by stands of ponderosa pines or pinyon juniper bushes, the brilliant red flowers almost explode from their surroundings. Look for hummingbirds busily pollinating this plant. Other species of penstemons that grow in the state are blue, lavender, or purple.

*Penstemon
eatonii*

Arrowleaf Balsam Root

other names: Bigroot, Big Sunflower
height: 10-20 inches
season: June-August

Don't confuse the arrowleaf balsam root with the true sunflower, which has several flower heads on each leafy stem. The balsam root's bright yellow flower head usually sits alone atop an almost leafless stalk. The leaves are arrow-shaped and up to twelve inches long, and they're covered with thick, silver-gray hairs. Native Americans used to eat the shoots and seeds of this plant. They also boiled, dried, and ground the roots to make a medicine. In the spring, elk and deer eat the young shoots, and bighorn sheep and horses like the leaves and flower heads.

*Balsamorhiza
sagittata*

Larkspur

other names: none
height: 12-18 inches
season: May-June

Larkspurs seldom grow near one another. Individual plants are usually found among clumps of grass or other flowers. This plant is poisonous to cattle and is the greatest cause of death among herds grazing on national forest land. Most deaths occur in early spring, before the plant blooms. Sheep are not affected by the plant, so they're often used to graze it off of ranch lands. Elk avoid the larkspur in the early spring when the leaves are forming, but they feed on it in late summer.

*Delphinium
nelsonii*

Blue Flax

other names: Lewis Flax, Prairie
  Flax
height: 8-24 inches
season: May-August

The stems of this plant are
made up of long, tough fibers
that are not easily broken. Native
Americans made cords and
fishing lines from them, and
relatives of this plant have been
used for thousands of years to
make linen. Even the wrapping
around Egyptian mummies was
made from a member of the flax
family. Linseed oil is extracted
from flax seed and used to make
paint, varnish, linoleum, and
printer's ink. Flax is also used as
a laxative, a salve for burns, and
a poultice. Blue flax can be fatal
to livestock.

*Linum
lewisii*

Hairy Golden Aster

other names: Goldeneye
height: 8-24 inches
season: late June-August

Feel this plant's silky-haired
leaves! While the flower looks
like an aster, technically it isn't.
The ray flowers of an aster are
white, purple, or blue. This plant
has yellow ray flowers and
yellow disk flowers. Look for this
plant in dry to medium-moist
soil in open areas, plains, sandy
river bottoms, valleys, hills, and
along roadsides.

Chrysopsis villosa

Broadleaf Yucca

other names: Spanish Bayonets,
  Soapweed
height: 2-3 feet
season: June-July

Native Americans had many
uses for the yucca. They ate its
flowers, fruit, and large black
seeds. They made baskets,
blankets, sandals, and cords from
the strong fibers of the stiff,
spiny leaves. And they made
soap and shampoo from the
crushed roots. The yucca has a
unique pollination partner.
Because the plant's pollen is
heavy and sticky rather than
powdery, it can't be scattered by
the wind. And a small, white,
night-flying moth called the
pronuba moth is the only insect
that can pollinate the yucca. The
female moth carries the pollen
from stamen to pistil. She also
lays her eggs in the yucca's
flowers.

*Yucca
baccata*

25

Rocky Mountain National Park

If you wanted to explore many different climates and habitats, you could spend your entire summer driving from Denver to the Arctic Circle. Or you could drive from Denver to the top of Trail Ridge Road in Rocky Mountain National Park. You'd see the same variety of zones. (The trip from Colorado Springs to the top of Pikes Peak will work, too.)

There are more than nine hundred plant species in this park. On these two pages are some of the most common and interesting varieties. Since the park includes the montane, subalpine, and alpine zones, be sure to look for the flowers listed in those sections of this book, too. The Indian paintbrush, described on page seven, is also found here.

To examine the tiny alpine flowers, get down on your hands and knees. Their intricate parts are amazing!

Golden Banner

other names: Golden Pea, False Lupine
height: 12-24 inches
season: June-July

It's easy to see the "banner," or uppermost petal, of this unusually shaped plant. Late in the summer, the golden banner forms long pea pods that contain its seeds. The entire plant is poisonous. Livestock and even insects avoid eating it. According to legend, the Pawnees used the golden banner to treat rheumatism. They burned the flowers and allowed the smoke to ease the pain.

Thermopsis divaricarpa

Little Red Elephants

other names: Elephant Heads
height: 6-24 inches
season: June-August

Little red elephant is the perfect name for this flower. It really looks like an elephant's head with big floppy ears and a long curling trunk. The odd shape helps bees to pollinate the flower more easily. When a bee lands, the flower smacks pollen onto the insect's belly. It's then picked up by the stigma of the next flower. The Latin name *Pedicularis* means "louse." It comes from an old belief that cattle and sheep would develop lice if they ate this plant. Elk like to graze on little red elephants in the early summer.

Pedicularis groenlandica

Alpine Avens

other names: none
height: 3-10 inches
season: June-August

Flies rather than bees are more likely to pollinate the alpine avens. The stamens and pistils (the pollen-bearing and pollen-receiving flower parts) are exposed so that pollen is easily transferred to and from a fly's body. The flower doesn't have a strong scent. This species, *rossii*, was named for James C. Ross, a nineteenth-century explorer.

Geum rossii

Mountain Gumweed

other names: none
height: 8-18 inches
season: July-September

If you like sticky goo, you'll love the mountain gumweed! The composite flowers open from ball-like buds covered with a gummy substance that discourages animals from eating them. Because gumweed is common, it was used a lot by early Native Americans to relieve nearly all bodily ills. They even chewed it like gum. *Don't* try this yourself, however. If the plant is growing in soil that contains selenium, the gumweed will be poisonous. Don't take a chance!

*Grindelia
subalpina*

Tall One-Sided Penstemon

other names: Beard Tongue
height: 2 feet
season: June-July

Penstemon is Greek for "five stamens." You can see them by peering into the tubular flower. Four of the stamens arch up along the inside of the tube like ribs of a whale. The fifth is sterile, lies along the bottom of the tube, and is often hairy. Since it looks like a hairy tongue, the plant is called beard tongue. Native Americans brewed medicines from this plant to cure a wide variety of ailments.

*Penstemon virgatus
ssp. asa-grayi*

Alpine Sunflower

other names: Old Man of the
   Mountain, Graylocks
height: 5-15 inches
season: June-July

Most sunflowers grow from a new seed every year. But the alpine sunflower stores energy in its roots for ten years or more until it has enough to produce its large flowers. Then it blooms only once, makes seeds, and dies. Unlike other sunflowers, this one doesn't rotate to face the sun moving across the sky. Instead, it always faces east, keeping its back to the strong west winds. On windy days, butterflies cling to the flower for protection. It's sometimes called old man of the mountain because of its white, woolly hair, which sheds wind, traps heat, reduces water loss, and protects the plant from the ultraviolet light of the high-altitude sun.

*Rydbergia grandiflora
Hymenoxys grandiflora*

Great Sand Dunes

Only four plants can grow here atop the trillions of tons of sand: the prairie sunflower, the scurfpea, and two grasses (Indian rice grass and blowout-grass). These hardy plants get their water from the moist sand below the surface. In turn, they provide shelter for insects and food for seed-eating rodents and birds.

Most visitors to the Great Sand Dunes National Monument come looking for fun. But when the sand gets too hot to enjoy, venture to the nearby foothills and mountains to look for more wildflowers, including prickly pear cactus, scarlet gilia, Rocky Mountain bee plant, and Indian paintbrush. All are described elsewhere in this book.

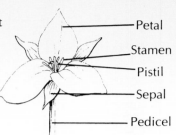

Petal
Stamen
Pistil
Sepal
Pedicel

Scurfpea	Prairie Sunflower
other names: Lemon Scurfpea height: 8 inches season: July-August	other names: Narrowleaf Sunflower height: 10-36 inches season: August-September

These tiny, purplish-blue blossoms, which resemble the sweetpea, survive in shifting sands in part because of their long underground stems, called rhizomes. These may extend many feet below the surface. The scurfpea takes root along the rhizome and sprouts above the sand. If a plant gets buried by sand, it simply sprouts another root system farther down the rhizome, sends up a new stem, and begins to bloom again. The leaflets smell like lemon.

The genus name *Helianthus* comes from two Greek words. *Helios* means "the sun," and *anthos* means "a flower." Behold! The sunflower! In late summer, this showy flower appears near the tops of the highest dunes. Like the scurfpea, which blooms earlier, this plant has adapted to life in the shifting sand, where the surface temperature can reach 140 degrees Fahrenheit. The prairie sunflower is also common in sandy soil on the plains.

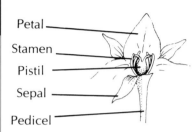

Petal
Stamen
Pistil
Sepal
Pedicel

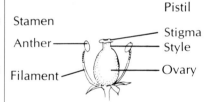

Pistil
Stamen
Anther
Filament
Stigma
Style
Ovary

Psoralea lanceolata

Helianthus petiolaris

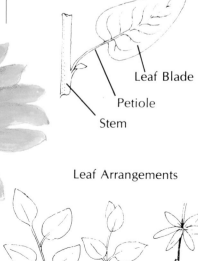

Leaf Blade
Petiole
Stem

Leaf Arrangements

Alternate   Opposite   Whorl

Glossary

Alternate	Not opposite each other
Annual	A plant that lives for one season
Anther	The part of the stamen containing pollen
Berry	A fleshy fruit containing seeds
Biennial	A plant that lives for two years
Bract	Leaflike scales
Bulb	A plant bud usually below the ground
Corm	A bulblike underground swelling of a stem
Composite	Flower heads composed of clusters of ray and disk flowers
Disk flower	Tubular florets in the center part of a composite flower head
Evergreen	Bearing green leaves or needles throughout the year
Filament	The stalk of the stamen
Floret	A small flower that is part of a cluster
Flower	Part of a plant containing male and/or female reproductive parts
Flower head	A dense cluster of flowers atop a stem
Fruit	A seed-bearing part of a plant
Habitat	The community where a plant naturally grows
Head	A dense cluster of flowers atop a stem
Herb	A seed plant with no woody tissue, whose stems die back to the ground each year
Irregular	Asymmetrical in shape
Nectar	Sweet liquid produced by flowers to attract insects
Opposite	Pairs of leaves opposite each other on a stem
Ovary	The part of the pistil that contains the developing seeds
Parasitic	Growing on and deriving nourishment from another plant
Pathfinders	Lines that guide insects to the nectar
Pedicel	The supporting stem of a single flower
Peduncle	The stalk of a flower or flower cluster
Perennial	A plant that lives from year to year
Petals	Floral leaves inside the sepals that attract pollinators
Petiole	The stem supporting a leaf
Pistil	The seed-bearing organ of a flower
Pollen	Powderlike cells produced by the stamens
Ray flower	The flowers around the edge of a flower head; each flower may resemble a single petal
Reflexed	Bent or curved backward or downward
Regular	Alike in size and shape
Rhizome	Underground stem or rootstock
Saprophyte	A plant that lives on dead organic matter
Seed	Developed female egg
Seed pod	Sack enclosing the developed female egg(s)
Sepal	The outermost floral leaf that protects the delicate petals
Shrub	Low woody plant, usually having several stems
Spadix	Fleshy spike that bears flowers
Spathe	Leafy covering connected to the base of a spadix
Spur	Hollow appendage of a petal or sepal
Stamen	Pollen-producing organ of a flower
Stigma	The end of the pistil that collects pollen
Style	The slender stalk of a pistil
Succulent	A plant with thick, fleshy leaves or stems that conserve moisture
Tendril	Slender, twining extension of a leaf or stem
Tepals	Petals and sepals that look alike
Tuber	A thickened underground stem having numerous buds
Whorl	Three or more leaves or branches growing from a common point

Where to See Wildflowers

Colorado offers many other excellent places to look for wildflowers. Some cities, parks, and monuments even sponsor hikes, workshops, or fireside talks with naturalists.

Here are some recommended places to view or learn about wildflowers. But don't restrict yourself to this list. Colorado is a wildflower heaven! You're likely to spot them almost anywhere you go.

In Denver:
Chatfield Arboretum, 9201 S. Carr St., Littleton, CO 80123, (303) 973-3705
Denver Botanic Gardens, 909 York St., Denver, CO 80206-3799, (303) 331-4000
Denver Museum of Natural History, 2001 Colorado Blvd., Denver, CO 80205,
    (303) 322-7009
Rocky Mountain Arsenal National Wildlife Area, Building 111,
    Commerce City, CO 80022-2180, (You *must* call ahead: (303) 289-0232)

National Parks and Forests:
Bent's Old Fort National Historic Site, 35110 Hwy. 194 E.,
    La Junta, CO 81050-9523, (719) 384-2596
Black Canyon of the Gunnison National Monument, 2233 E. Main St., Suite A,
    Montrose, CO 81401, (303) 249-7036
Colorado National Monument, Fruita, CO 81521-0001, (303) 858-3617
Comanche National Grassland, P.O. Box 127, 27162 Hwy. 287, Springfield, CO 81073,
    (719) 523-6591
Curecanti National Recreation Area, 102 Elk Creek, Gunnison, CO 81230, (303) 641-0406
Dinosaur National Monument, P.O. Box 210, Dinosaur, CO 81610-0210, (303) 374-2216
Florissant Fossil Beds National Monument, P.O. Box 185, Florissant, CO 80816-0185,
    (719) 748-3253
Great Sand Dunes National Monument, 11500 Hwy. 150, Mosca, CO 81146,
    (719) 378-2312
Hovenweep National Monument, McElmo Route, Cortez, CO 81321, (303) 529-4461
Mesa Verde National Park, CO 81330, (303) 529-4475
Pawnee National Grasslands, 660 "O" St., Suite A, Greeley, CO 80613, (303) 353-5004
Rocky Mountain National Park, Estes Park, CO 80517, (303) 586-2371

For information on any of Colorado's twelve national forests, contact USDA Forest
    Service, Rocky Mountain Region, 740 Sims St., Lakewood, CO 80225, (303) 275-5370

Natural Areas:
Bear Creek Regional Park Nature Center, southwest of Colorado Springs
Golden Gate State Park, north of Golden
Handies Peak, southwest of Lake City
Hunter-Frying Pan Wilderness Area, east of Aspen
Maroon Bells-Snowmass Wilderness Area, southwest of Aspen
Mount Massive Wilderness Area, west of Leadville
Mueller Ranch State Park, west of Colorado Springs
Pikes Peak, west of Colorado Springs
Red Rocks Park, north of Morrison
South San Juan Wilderness Area, east of Pagosa Springs

Index